Plate 2

Plate 3

Plate 4

do not cut out
white areas between
arms and body

Plate 5

do not cut out
white area between
arm and body

Plate 6

Plate 7

do not cut out
white areas between
arms and body

Plate 8

Cut out shape above.
Glue edge to back of hat at left,
forming a pocket; let dry.
Slip doll's head into pocket.

Plate 9

do not cut out
white areas between
arms and bodies

Plate 10

Cut out shape above.
Glue edge to back of hat at left,
forming a pocket; let dry.
Slip doll's head into pocket.

Plate 11

do not cut out
white area between
arm and body

Plate 12

Cut out shape above. Glue edge to back of hat at right, forming a pocket; let dry. Slip doll's head into pocket.

Plate 13

Cut out shape above.
Glue edge to back of hat at left,
forming a pocket; let dry.
Slip doll's head into pocket.

do not cut out
white area between
arm and body

Plate 14

Cut out shape above.
Glue edge to back of hat
at right, forming a pocket;
let dry. Slip doll's head
into pocket.

Plate 15